JANET'S JUICE BOOK

JANET'S JUICE BOOK

Great New Recipes for the Juicer and Blender

Janet Hazen

Photographs by Joyce Oudkerk Pool

Food Styling by Robert Burns

CHRONICLE BOOKS

SAN FRANCISCO

Library of Congress Cataloging-in-Publication Data

Hazen, Janet.
  [Juice book]
  Janet's juice book : great new recipes for the juicer and
  blender / by Janet Hazen ; photography by Joyce
  Oudkerk Pool.
     p.   cm.
  ISBN 0-8118-0309-0
  1. Fruit drinks.   2. Vegetable juices.   I. Title.
TX815.H29   1993
641.8'75—dc20   92-28094
                                                 CIP

Printed in Japan.

Distributed in Canada by Raincoast Books,
112 East Third Ave., Vancouver, B.C. V5T 1C8

10 9 8 7 6 5 4 3 2 1

Chronicle Books
275 Fifth Street
San Francisco, CA 94103

Contents

CREATIVE JUICES

Many Americans associate juice with the solid tubes of frozen orange juice concentrate found in the freezer section of their grocery store. Most of us grew up starting off our day sipping chilled glasses of reconstituted beverage at the kitchen table, occasionally varying the routine with something "exotic," like canned tomato juice or frozen grapefruit juice.

But why limit ourselves? In contrast to the limited range of commercially prepared juices, the world of fresh juice is broad and expansive. Creamy smooth pineapple-mango juice with a blush of raspberry; fresh, sweet tomato-carrot juice laced with red bell pepper; ripe summer peaches blended with banana and luscious yogurt are just three examples of what you can make from this collection of juice and blender-drink recipes.

With the current focus on fresh, natural, light, and lean foods, it's only natural that freshly made vegetable and fruit drinks have become a popular part of the culinary scene. Although the recipes in this book were designed with flavor, texture, and aroma in mind, their innate health benefits are an obvious part of their charm.

Ninety-five percent of the nutrients in a given fruit or vegetable are found in the juice. Liquids extracted from fresh, wholesome, ripe fruits and vegetables form a vital part of a balanced, healthy diet and are an important, easy-to-make source of vitamins and minerals. They are also one of the quickest ways to ingest nutrients—the essence of sun-drenched produce, taken in liquid form, is rapidly absorbed into the blood stream. Although it is important to include at least four or five servings of whole fruit and vegetables in your diet each day, when you consider that 1 cup of carrot juice contains the nutrient equivalent of four cups of raw carrots, the rewards of drinking fresh juices become apparent.

In this era of heightened nutrition consciousness, we are all interested in eating "live" foods—foods that come straight from the earth, that are grown with a minimum of chemicals, that are prepared without pasteurizing, additives or chemical treatment. When you make your own juices, you have complete control over what goes into them—you select the produce and decide whether to use sugar, salt, or other flavoring agents.

Latin American, African, Caribbean, and Southeast Asian countries have always included fresh vegetable and fruit juices in their diets. After all, aren't they a logical result of an abundance of fresh produce bursting with goodness and flavor? In most of these countries it is commonplace to enjoy at least two or three glasses of fresh orange, banana, mango, papaya, carrot, or tomato juice on a daily basis.

Though here in America we may not have fresh fruit and vegetable vendors on every street corner, as a result of modern growing and shipping techniques, we do have stores and farmer's markets offering a dazzling variety of seasonal produce for us to use in creating our own juices.

Juice and blender drinks are one of the least intimidating preparations to make at home. An electric juicer, a blender, a few sharp knives, a cutting board, and a few other basic items are the only equipment needed. The rest is up to you. You may not feel the need to follow recipes to create a delicious and restorative beverage, but in case you have depleted your reservoir of recipes or feel insecure about the process, the recipes in this book will serve as a source of inspiration to guide you.

This book is divided into two sections; the first is devoted to vegetable and fruit juices, the second to blender drinks. A wide variety of vegetables and fruits are used in the juice section, but because I feel fruits are particularly well suited to the blender, you will find only fruit-based beverages in the blender-drink section.

Although drinking fresh juices is a natural, pure, invigorating way to absorb vitamins and minerals, I don't for a minute reject the notion of using some of these mixtures to enhance a wide variety of culinary delights—use them as the base for summer cocktails, in soups and marinades, or as savory or sweet dessert sauces, for example.

Making a beverage from pure, live foods is a natural and safe alternative to guzzling a can of soda loaded with sugar or chemicals . . . or both. But this book is not meant as a serious tool for rigorous dieting, fasting, or health remedies. I do not take a political, medical, or moral stand on incorporating fresh vegetable and fruit juices in my diet—I simply feel better when I drink these wonderful, fresh beverages, and I give enormous pleasure to my taste buds at the same time! After experimenting with some of the recipes in this book, I hope you will share my delight in these liquid creations.

List of Recipes

Kiwi-Apple-Strawberry Juice

Kiwi-Peach-Grapefruit Juice

Pineapple-Pear-Cherry Juice

Cherry-Tangerine-Lime Juice

Watermelon-Strawberry-Red Grape Juice

Watermelon-Raspberry-Apple Juice

Watermelon-Cherry-Nectarine Juice

Five-Fruit Juice

Strawberry-Apple-Tangerine Juice

Peach-Blueberry-Tangerine Juice

Strawberry-Apple-Pineapple Juice

Peach-Plum-Apricot Juice

Carrot-Green Pepper-Fennel-Bean Sprout Juice

Carrot-Bean Sprout-Celery-Jalapeño Juice

Snap Pea-Celery-Sprout Juice

Fennel-Cucumber-Sprout Juice

Nectarine-Strawberry-Orange Juice

Grape-Apple-Pear Juice

Watermelon-Nectarine-Pear Juice

Cantaloupe-Mango Juice

Pineapple-Peach-Apple Juice

Mango-Pineapple-Peach Juice

Plum-Apple-Grape Juice

Fennel-Grape-Cucumber Juice

Celery-Green Pepper-Parsley-Carrot Juice

Carrot-Beet-Celery-Tomato Juice

Carrot-Tomato-Fennel-Lettuce Juice

Blender Drinks

Strawberry-Tangerine-Pear Nectar

Strawberry-Banana-Lemon Nectar

Raspberry-Strawberry-Peach Nectar

Strawberry-Orange-Mango Nectar

Raspberry-Blackberry-Orange Nectar

Yellow Cherry-Papaya-Nectarine Cooler

Honeydew Melon-Apricot-Nectarine Fizz

Nectarine-Apricot-Banana Nectar

Nectarine-Plum-Peach Juice

Nectarine-Peach-Apricot-Lime Nectar

Banana-Peach-Nectarine Smoothie

Papaya-Banana-Pineapple Fizz

Papaya-Watermelon-Lime Cooler

Peach-Plum-Ginger Cooler

Blackberry-Apricot-Pineapple Cooler

Banana-Pineapple Smoothie with Blueberries

Banana-Kiwi-Orange Nectar

Apricot-Tangerine Smoothie

Apricot-Banana-Honeydew Melon Nectar

Tangerine-Raspberry-Cantaloupe Smoothie

Orange-Pineapple-Raspberry Fizz

Cantaloupe-Orange-Papaya Smoothie

Cantaloupe-Nectarine-Date Nectar

Peach-Grape Nectar

Peach-Grapefruit-Banana Nectar

Banana-Papaya-Lemon Cooler

Pineapple-Banana-Tangerine Nectar

Mango-Peach Smoothie

Papaya-Tangerine Nectar

Cantaloupe-Peach-Strawberry Nectar

Tangerine-Nectarine-Strawberry Fizz

Banana-Nectarine-Apricot-Tangerine Nectar

Kiwi-Honeydew Melon Nectar

Blueberry-Banana-Date-Lemon Fizz

Blueberry-Blackberry-Peach Nectar

Blueberry-Kiwi-Peach Nectar

Cherry-Pear-Peach Nectar

Honeydew Melon-Peach-Apricot Smoothie

Apricot-Raspberry-Cherry Smoothie

Apricot-Orange-Pear Cooler

Basic Techniques for Making Juices and Blender Drinks

Equipment

Preparing fruit and vegetable drinks in a blender or juicer is one of the easiest things to do in a kitchen. This is one food preparation that doesn't require any secret tricks or culinary skills; all that is required is the produce, the machine, and a few cooking utensils.

The basic equipment needed for extracting the liquids from fruits and vegetables is, of course, an electric juicer. There are many from which to choose, so do a little research and pick the juicer that is right for you. I recommend using a juicer that has a separate compartment for collecting the pulp that is extracted from the produce. This feature and a high-power motor are the two most important components of an electric juicer. Of course, a juicer with more horsepower is also going to be more expensive; only you can be the judge of which machine is right for your purposes.

In addition to the juicer, you will want a cutting board, a couple of sharp knives, a 4-cup glass measuring cup, and perhaps a lettuce spinner for drying greens and herbs after they have been washed. Aside from a blender, all that you will need when making blender drinks is a small, hand-held strainer, a cutting board, and sharp knives.

The operating principles of an electric juicer are straightforward: After they are inserted into a food tube, pieces of fruit or vegetable are forced against a sharp, rotating stainless blade and are essentially ground to a pulp. This action releases the juices of the fruits and vegetables. The pulp, fiber, skins, seeds, and stems are forced into a separate unit, and in the case of older or less expensive machines, into a circular barrel around the blade. The juice is filtered and released through a spout on the exterior of the machine.

The pulp should be removed from the machine as it accumulates; some older machines will

◄ Apple-Blackberry-Blueberry Juice

have a difficult time extracting juice if there is too much pulp in the barrel. It is also important to clean the juicer when you have finished making juice for the day, or if you are switching from vegetables to fruits. In general, follow the manufacturer's operating instructions for your juicer because they vary among different models.

Unlike juicers, the action of rotating blades at the bottom of a blender crushes the entire fruit or vegetable, rather than extracting its juices and separating it from the pulp. Whole foods, if they are soft or contain enough liquids, will be pulverized within seconds in a good-quality blender. When the desired consistency is achieved, the mixture is removed from the blender and transferred to an appropriate vessel. The inside of the blender can be scraped with a rubber spatula to help remove what remains on the sides of the container and around the blades. It is a good idea to wash and dry the blender when you are finished so it is ready to use again.

Purchasing Produce

Any wholesome, ripe piece of fruit or vegetable is suitable for use when making juices or blender drinks. It is preferable to use organic or pesticide-free produce, and I like to buy as many fruits and vegetables from the farmer's market as possible because I know they're fresh. Making juices is also one way to enjoy the bounty of your own vegetable garden or fruit tree. At the grocery store you may be able to find discounted produce that is marred or visually undesirable, but otherwise perfect for consumption; picture-perfect apples, carrots, tomatoes, and squash aren't necessary for making juice! It's a good idea to take a few minutes to wash and dry your purchases when you get home from shopping. Any time you have the urge to make a juice or blender drink, all you'll have to do is cut the fruits or vegetables and put them through the machine. I recommend drying leafy greens and herbs in a lettuce spinner and storing them in plastic bags in the refrigerator. I like to store most fruits and vegetables at cool room temperature, but some delicate and perishable items such as berries, grapes, leafy greens, celery,

cucumbers, herbs, and summer squashes should be stored in the refrigerator if you can't use them within one day. Sturdy vegetables such as broccoli, cauliflower, and root vegetables are not harmed by chilling and can be refrigerated for up to 2 weeks if wrapped tightly in plastic bags. However, tomatoes, peaches, plums, nectarines, apricots, bananas, melons, mangoes, papayas, kiwis, apples, pears, and citrus fruits are much better when stored at cool room temperature. Most fruits and vegetables are easier to juice when they are not cold; the same is true when making blender drinks.

Preparing Fruits and Vegetables

Although many fruits and vegetables do not require any special treatment prior to being juiced or put in the blender, there are some guidelines to keep in mind.

For juicers: Obviously, all fruits and vegetables with hard or inedible skins—melons, citrus,

pineapple, mango, papaya, and kiwi, for example —must be peeled before placing in a juicer.

Some very powerful and expensive juicers can handle melon rinds, but I recommend removing them in all cases. Some juice books suggest peeling citrus fruits—oranges, tangerines, limes, lemons, and grapefruits—and placing the entire fruits, membrane and all, in the juicer. Certainly, more valuable vitamins (including bioflavinoids) will be saved using this method, but I find the resulting juice too pulpy and acrid

for my taste. Instead, I squeeze the juice by hand or with a manual juicer. Because of this preference, the recipes in this book call for citrus juice that is squeezed separately, then added to the other ingredients after they are processed in the juicer. This is a personal choice, however; I suggest trying a juice both ways before making a decision.

All fruits with pits, such as nectarines, peaches, apricots, plums, and cherries, must be pitted before juicing. Although most pits can be removed with the aid of a paring knife, the only sensible way to remove pits from cherries is with a cherry pitter. This handy little device can be purchased at any cookware shop and in the cookware section of most department stores. It may seem like a lot of work, but the few minutes it takes to pit a cup of cherries is well worth the terrific cherry juice you will enjoy drinking.

In addition to these preparations, fruits and vegetables must be cut small enough to fit through the feed tube of a juicer.

For blenders: Because blenders simply purée ingredients without extracting anything, in addition to removing hard or inedible skins and pits from all fruits and vegetables, as you would for juicing, you must also remove the cores, stems, and large seeds from fruit and vegetables. In addition, it's best to coarsely chop foods into about 1-inch pieces before putting them into the blender.

Before juicing and blending, I suggest cutting all the food that will be used to make the beverage. Then lay the cut and prepared produce on a cutting board next to the juicer or blender and begin making your beverage. Be sure to have a container large enough to collect all the juice as it comes out of the spout of the juicer. I like to use a 4-cup glass measuring cup.

Juicing Techniques

When preparing a juice with several different ingredients of different textures it is best to alternate harder items with softer ones. For example, when making a juice of two hard root vegetables such as carrots and parsnips, and a softer type of produce, such as tomatoes, begin with the parsnips, juice the tomato second, and finish with the carrots. Alternating soft with hard cleans the blades between the vegetables and enables the juicer to extract as much juice

from each vegetable as possible. When using herbs, sprouts, or small leafy greens you may want to wrap them in a large lettuce or Swiss chard leaf, or force them through the feed tube between two pieces of firmer vegetable.

All fruits and vegetables produce different amounts of liquids. There are even variables within the same group; one batch of tomatoes could yield more juice than another batch. If you have a very powerful and expensive juicer, you may have a higher yield of juice than if using a lesser-quality machine. The yields vary from juicer to fruit to vegetable, but since recipes

aren't exact, and juice making is not a science, the precise quantities of any given juice are not crucial to the success of a particular beverage.

Blending Techniques

Most fruits and vegetables can be placed in the blender, puréed to a pleasing consistency and enjoyed immediately. There are a few beverages, however, that require straining after they are puréed. These include drinks that call for berries with seeds: blackberries, strawberries, raspberries, boysenberries, and in some cases blueberries. Drinks that include fruits with a great deal of sinewy fiber such as pineapples and mangoes are also more palatable when strained after puréeing. This is one more step, but the result-

ing smooth texture makes it well worth the minute it takes to strain a beverage through a wire sieve.

When a recipe calls for the addition of ice, it's important to crush the ice slightly before adding it to the blender. Most blenders can't handle whole ice cubes, therefore I suggest placing the cubes between two kitchen towels and crushing them with a heavy hammer or cast iron pot. Add the crushed ice cubes just before serving, otherwise the ice will melt and the slushy, chilled effect may be ruined.

Substitutions

If you are ready to make a particular recipe and suddenly find that you have nectarines instead of peaches, go ahead and make the juice with nectarines! These formulas aren't written in granite, nor are there any precise, strict rules for making beverages of this sort. Many fruits are interchangeable: nectarines and peaches; peaches and apricots; blackberries and boysenberries; oranges and tangerines; honeydew melon and crenshaw; yellow and red plums; and limes and lemons. Of course, the taste won't be exactly the same if you substitute one fruit for another, but you may like the results even better.

Beyond the Basics: Inventing Your Own Juices

Creating your own recipe for a blender drink or juice isn't difficult. If you've been making your own natural vegetable and fruit juices and blender drinks for a while then you know how simple it is to invent new combinations. Taste, color, texture, and ingredient preferences are a personal thing, and like other foods and pre-

pared dishes, a predilection for certain flavor pairings is natural.

This collection of recipes just touches on some of the innumerable combinations that are possible. My hope is that you can use these recipes as inspiration for creating more concoctions on your own. Just think about some of your favorite flavors and foods—would they work well

together or would they clash? Some assertive flavors cancel out the more delicate and subtle tones of fruits and vegetables, so these pairings wouldn't make sense. Think about different textures and the moisture content of produce; it's a good idea to pair starchy, pulpy ingredients with those high in moisture. Color is another consideration. When I developed these recipes I thought about the appearance of the final product as much as possible. It would be fickle and silly to only create beverages that are attractive to the eye, but by the same token, who wants to guzzle down a glass of gray, murky sludge?

In general, foods that grow together go together; this is true when cooking and pre-

paring meals as well. Summer fruits such as plums, apricots, peaches, nectarines, berries, and melons pair nicely with one another, and the fall / winter fruits such as apples, pears, tangerines, citrus, and pomegranates are good companions.

This doesn't mean however, that fruits of different seasons, like apples and peaches, can't be combined. Experiment! In addition, keep in mind that tropical fruits such as pineapples, mangoes, papayas, bananas, and guavas are terrific when combined in juices or blender drinks. Don't forget about dates—they add a luxurious sweetness and interesting texture to most blender drinks. Any fruit that you particularly adore can go into your next drink. You may choose one fruit as the backbone of the beverage and include one or two highlight fruits to add a flavor punch or dramatic color. Perhaps a happy melding of three equal portions of three distinct fruits is what you're after, or maybe it's just one primary flavor accented with a splash of citrus to help bring out its natural essence and sweetness.

When creating vegetable juices, ask yourself if you would enjoy the flavor of a particular vegetable in its raw state. In many cases, uncooked vegetables have a much more assertive flavor, and some folks find this objectionable. For example, although some like the taste of cooked beets drizzled with olive oil and sprinkled with salt and pepper, would they find the flavor of raw beet juice appealing? To some it may be terrific; to others it might be too strong. Tomatoes, cucumbers, celery, and carrots have the mildest flavors of the vegetable juices, so if you want to experiment with a new vegetable, and aren't sure if you will like the results, you may want to use one or two of these as the predominant background flavor for the one you are trying out.

After all is said and done, and you manage to create a beverage you just don't like, it's not a catastrophe! It isn't as though you have spent tremendous amounts of money, time, and energy shopping at many stores, following a long, complex recipe, and cooking over the hot stove all day—it's probably less than one dollar and a few minutes you've spent learning something new about food, combining ingredients, and your personal taste. You'll probably stumble upon your favorite combination of flavors in your next attempt!

1. Vegetable and Fruit Juices

Vegetables and fruits suitable for using in a juicer include those with a high moisture content or fibrous, pulpy flesh. Good-tasting fruits and vegetables are also likely candidates, but bitter or bland-tasting varieties often can be combined with sweeter or more assertively flavored ones to produce a rewarding and tasty juice.

All root vegetables, such as carrots, parsnips, turnips, rutabagas, potatoes—both white and sweet—and beets, work very well in a juicer. Personally, I'm not terribly interested in juices made from the strong, cabbage-family vegetables such as broccoli, cauliflower, and brussels sprouts, but these flavorful vegetables are favored by some. Leafy green vegetables such as cabbage, spinach, kale, chard, and mustard greens can also be put through a juicer; they yield dark green, pungent juice very high in vitamins and minerals. These liquids taste best when mixed with larger proportions of milder liquids extracted from carrots, beets, tomatoes, or cucumbers. Tomatoes, cucumbers, celery, and green and red bell peppers are some of the more popular, pleasant vegetables used for making healthful concoctions. These serve best as a backbone for other, more definite flavors or for forming the bulk of a juice that will be highlighted with just a touch of juice from a low-moisture vegetable. A minimal amount of liquid can be extracted from small vegetables like string beans, snow peas, and green peas. Eggplant and mushrooms can be avoided altogether because their taste and color are unpleasant and / or their juices are undigestible.

In general, it's best not to combine vegetables and fruits in the same beverage. While some people have no problem digesting both at once, many may suffer from unpleasant bloating, intestinal gas, or mild stomach cramps if they combine large amounts of vegetables and fruits in the same meal. Likewise, juices made from leafy green vegetables such as watercress, cabbage, spinach, kale, chard, or parsley should be combined with three times as much juice made from carrots, cucumbers, tomatoes, or some other non-green vegetable. This is not just for

improving taste; an overdose of leafy greens can cause mild intestinal discomfort.

Fruits with a high moisture content can be put through a juicer with excellent results. Among the fruits most commonly used for juicing are apples, pears, mangoes, papayas, pineapple, plums, apricots, peaches, strawberries, blackberries, blueberries, raspberries, nectarines, grapes, melons, and kiwis. As I mentioned in "Techniques," many people process citrus fruits such as grapefruit, tangerines, oranges, lemons, and limes in juicers, but I find the results too bitter and pulpy. Due to their starchy makeup, bananas also cannot be successfully juiced, but they are just terrific when whirled in the blender with other fruits.

Accent produce such as limes and lemons, ginger and garlic, and jalapeño and serrano chilies are useful when you want to add zest or a specific highlight to a juice. Bear in mind however, a little bit of raw ginger, garlic, or hot chili goes a long way, especially when introduced to a liquid medium.

Remember, fruits and vegetables with hard or inedible skins must be peeled before juicing, and fruits with stones must be pitted (see Techniques, page 17).

Juices are best when sipped at room temperature immediately after they are made. I don't recommend storing freshly made juices in the refrigerator for more than 30 minutes—the vitamins and minerals are at their peak as soon as the juice is extracted from the vegetable or fruit. However, if you prefer colder juices, pour them over ice.

The recipes in this section yield one or two portions of juice—about 2½ cups per recipe. This is the average portion size for two people (about 10 ounces per person), but it would be sufficient served as a small taste for three or four people. Certainly, all of the recipes can be doubled or tripled with success.

Apple-Carrot Juice

When it comes to fresh juice, this is surely one of the most popular fruit-vegetable combinations. You can vary the amounts of either the apples or carrots to make the juice sweeter or more savory.

Makes about 2 cups.

4 apples, cut into wedges
3 carrots, trimmed

Process the apples and carrots in a juicer. Mix well and serve immediately.

Apple-Peach-Nectarine Juice

What better way to eat an apple a day? Be sure to select peaches and nectarines that are juicy-ripe.

Makes about 2 cups.

1 apple, cut into wedges
3 peaches, pitted and cut into wedges
1 nectarine, pitted and cut into wedges

Process the apple, peaches, and nectarine in a juicer. Mix well and serve immediately.

Apple-Blackberry-Blueberry Juice

Deep violet and bursting with the flavors of summer berries, this intense juice makes an excellent afternoon pick-me-up, and it is also delicious when frozen slightly and served as a "slush."

Makes about 2¼ cups.

2 large apples, cut into wedges
2 cups blackberries
2 cups blueberries

Process the apples, blackberries, and blueberries in a juicer. Mix well and serve immediately.

Pear-Blackberry-Red Grape Juice

Luscious and thick, this unusual juice is very filling and satisfying, and it is an ideal beverage to serve when trying to avoid eating a fattening snack in the middle of the afternoon.

Makes about 3 cups.

2 pears, cut into wedges
1 cup blackberries
2½ cups red grapes

Process the pears, blackberries, and grapes in a juicer. Mix well and serve immediately.

Pear-Plum-Grape Juice

For a pale green-colored beverage, choose plump, sugary yellow plums and green grapes; for a rose-tinted juice, use red plums and red grapes. In either case, buy ripe, flavorful produce at the peak of the season.

Makes about 2½ cups.

2 pears, cut into wedges
4 plums, pitted and cut into wedges
1 cup grapes (green or red)

Process the pears, plums, and grapes in a juicer. Mix well and serve immediately.

Pear-Apple-Ginger Juice

Spicy and heartwarming, I would serve this juice when the fall leaves begin to turn, when apples and pears are at their peak. For a unique alcoholic beverage, try adding a jigger of light rum to this concoction.

Makes about 2½ cups.

4 pears, cut into wedges
2 apples, cut into wedges
½-inch piece fresh gingerroot

Process the pears, apples, and ginger in a juicer. Mix well and serve immediately.

Tomato-Carrot-Celery-Lime Juice

Distinctive and tart, the essence of each vegetable and fruit comes through in this lively juice.

Makes about 3 cups.

2 large tomatoes, cut into wedges
1 large carrot, trimmed
2 stalks celery, trimmed
¼ cup freshly squeezed lime juice (about 3 limes)

Process the tomatoes, carrot, and celery in a juicer. Add the lime juice and mix well. Serve immediately.

Tomato-Carrot-Garlic-Parsley Juice

Startlingly delicious, this deep-red potion has a robust flavor and is excellent used as a base for hot or chilled soups, or as a marinade for meat or poultry.

Makes about 2½ cups.

3 large tomatoes, cut into wedges
2 carrots, trimmed
1 clove garlic, peeled
1 medium bunch parsley

Process the tomatoes, carrots, garlic, and parsley in a juicer. Mix well and serve immediately.

Tomato-Carrot-Red Pepper Juice

Robust, healthful, and very high in vitamin C, this deep orange- colored juice is unique and tasty. You could use this juice as a base for a chilled summer soup, or combine it with tomato soup to add depth of flavor.

Makes about 3 cups.

3 large tomatoes, cut into wedges
2 carrots, trimmed
2 red peppers, cut into wedges

Process the tomatoes, carrots, and red peppers in a juicer. Mix well and serve immediately.

Tomato-Celery-Green Pepper Juice

This distinctive juice is reminiscent of the popular chilled Spanish soup called gazpacho, and although it would make an excellent base for Bloody Marys, it is wonderful on its own.

Makes about 3 cups.

3 large tomatoes, cut into wedges
2 stalks celery, trimmed
1 large green pepper, cut into wedges

Process the tomatoes, celery, and green pepper in a juicer. Mix well and serve immediately.

Tomato-Cucumber-Jalapeño Juice

If you enjoy sizzling hot chili peppers, you may want to increase the number of jalapeños in this recipe. Add some celery salt, Worcestershire sauce, a teaspoon of horseradish, and a shot of vodka to make an excellent Bloody Mary.

Makes about 2¼ cups.

3 large tomatoes, cut into wedges
1 large cucumber, peeled and cut into wedges
2 jalapeño peppers, stemmed

Process the tomatoes, cucumber, and jalapeño peppers in a juicer. Mix well and serve immediately.

Cucumber-Celery-Green Pepper-Fennel Juice

The refreshing flavors of four vegetables make a soothing, pale green juice, perfect for an afternoon energizer.

Makes about 2 cups.

2 large cucumbers, peeled and cut into wedges
4 stalks celery, trimmed
1 large green pepper, cut into wedges
1 bulb fennel, trimmed and cut into wedges

Process the cucumbers, celery, green pepper, and fennel in a juicer. Mix well and serve immediately.

Cucumber-Parsley-Carrot Juice

Frankly, this isn't the most attractive juice in this collection, but its restorative qualities and healthy flavor make up for its rather dull color.

Makes about 2 cups.

1 large cucumber, peeled and cut into wedges
1 large bunch parsley
3 carrots, trimmed

Process the cucumber, parsley, and carrots in a juicer. Mix well and serve immediately.

Cantaloupe-Carrot-Lemon Juice

This delightful, pleasant, melon-based juice is wonderful first thing in the morning. I prefer the more complex flavors of Meyer lemons for this soft orange-colored beverage, but any variety of fresh lemon will be just fine. Try adding a dash of cayenne pepper for an unusual accent.

Makes about 3 cups.

3 cups peeled and coarsely chopped cantaloupe
    (1 very large cantaloupe)
2 large carrots, trimmed
¼ cup freshly squeezed Meyer lemon juice
    (about 3 lemons)

Process the cantaloupe and carrots in a juicer. Add the lemon juice and mix well. Serve immediately.

Cantaloupe-Apple-Strawberry Juice

The mild flavor and silky texture of cantaloupe provide the perfect backdrop for the flavors of apple and strawberry in this rosy juice. This subtle beverage would be appealing to children or those with sensitive palates.

Makes about 3 cups.

1½ cups peeled and coarsely chopped cantaloupe
    (about half of a small cantaloupe)
2 apples, cut into wedges
8 large strawberries

Process the cantaloupe, apples, and strawberries in a juicer. Mix well and drink immediately.

Pineapple-Honeydew Melon-Strawberry Juice

This luscious juice is naturally sweet and tastes of summer. It is excellent in the morning served with a bowl of yogurt and fresh berries.

Makes about 3 cups.

*1½ cups peeled and coarsely chopped pineapple
   (about half of a small pineapple)
2 cups peeled and coarsely chopped honeydew melon
   (about half of a medium melon)
1 cup strawberries*

Process the pineapple, melon, and strawberries in a juicer. Mix well and serve immediately.

Pineapple-Mango-Raspberry Juice

Tropical and sweet, this thick fruit juice is filling and delicious. Double the recipe and serve in your favorite glass pitcher for a stunning opener to a Sunday brunch.

Makes about 3 cups.

*2 cups peeled and coarsely chopped pineapple
   (about half of a large pineapple)
2 mangoes, peeled, pitted, and cut into wedges
1 cup raspberries*

Process the pineapple, mangoes, and raspberries in a juicer. Mix well and serve immediately.

Celery-Sweet Potato-Carrot-Ginger Juice

Although the addition of sweet potato may seem unappealing, the flavor of this sweet, brick-colored juice is elusive, unexpected, and surprisingly delicious.

Makes about 2 cups.

4 stalks celery, trimmed
1 large sweet potato, cut into wedges
2 carrots, trimmed
½-inch piece fresh gingerroot

Process the celery, sweet potato, carrots, and ginger in a juicer. Mix well and serve immediately.

Celery-Fennel-Apple Juice

Light, fragrant, and very unusual, this subtle juice makes a pleasant before-dinner beverage in warm weather.

Makes about 2 cups.

3 stalks celery, trimmed
1 bulb fennel, trimmed and cut into wedges
1 apple, cut into wedges

Process the celery, fennel, and apple in a juicer. Mix well and serve immediately.

Apple-Carrot-Beet Juice

Creamy and simple, this lovely, pale, orangish pink juice combines two of my favorite vegetables with sweet apples to make a pleasing beverage. This juice is ideal for those who love the earthy flavor of beets.

Makes about 2 cups.

2 apples, cut into wedges
2 large carrots, trimmed
4 small red beets, trimmed and cut into wedges

Process the apples, carrots, and beets in a juicer. Mix well and serve immediately.

Beet-Carrot-Orange Juice

This citrus-accented juice is a good any-time-of-day tonic that is loaded with valuable vitamins and minerals. For a more assertive flavor, substitute grapefruit juice for the orange juice.

Makes about 2 cups.

3 medium beets, trimmed and cut into wedges
2 carrots, trimmed
1 cup freshly squeezed orange juice (3 to 4 oranges)

Process the beets and the carrots in a juicer. Add the orange juice and mix well. Drink immediately.

Beet-Raspberry-Celery Juice

These three ingredients are components of one of my favorite salads, so I decided to put them together in liquid form. The resulting juice is both sweet and savory, the celery tempers the robust flavor of beets, and raspberries add sweetness. This juice is deep red and makes a stunning presentation.

Makes about 1½ cups.

8 small red beets, trimmed and cut into wedges
2 cups raspberries
3 stalks celery, trimmed

Process the beets, raspberries, and celery in a juicer. Mix well and serve immediately.

Kiwi-Grape-Honeydew Melon Juice

Sweet, light, and very fresh-tasting, this lovely pale green juice makes a soothing morning beverage that's perfect on a hot summer day.

Makes about 2½ cups.

4 kiwis, peeled and cut into wedges
2 cups green grapes
1½ cups peeled and coarsely chopped honeydew
  melon (about half of a small melon)

Process the kiwi, grapes, and melon in a juicer. Mix well and serve immediately.

Kiwi-Apple-Strawberry Juice

The essence of each fruit comes through in this clean-tasting, pale pink juice. Feel free to substitute your favorite seasonal berry for the strawberries.

Makes about 2½ cups.

1 kiwi, peeled and cut into wedges
2 apples, cut into wedges
10 large strawberries

Process the kiwi, apples, and strawberries in a juicer. Mix well and serve immediately.

Kiwi-Peach-Grapefruit Juice

The soft flavors of peach, the neutral, sweet flavors of kiwi, and the sharp taste of grapefruit make a palate-awakening drink that is good any time you need an uplifting refresher.

Makes about 2½ cups.

1 kiwi, peeled and cut into wedges
2 large peaches, pitted and cut into wedges
1 cup freshly squeezed grapefruit juice
  (about 2 grapefruits)

Process the kiwi and peaches in a juicer. Add the grapefruit juice and mix well. Serve immediately.

Pineapple-Pear-Cherry Juice

Sweet, fragrant, and rose-colored, this juice is wonderful served over ice on a hot afternoon. Be sure to choose a ripe, aromatic pineapple for this recipe.

Makes about 3 cups.

*1½ cups peeled and coarsely chopped pineapple
    (about half of a small pineapple)
2 pears, cut into wedges
1 cup pitted cherries*

Process the pineapple, pears, and cherries in a juicer. Mix well and serve immediately, or pour over ice for a chilled beverage.

Cherry-Tangerine-Lime Juice

Tart and reviving, this ruby red juice is terrific as is, but it also makes a snappy and unique cocktail when combined with tequila over ice.

Makes about 2 cups.

*2 cups pitted cherries
¾ cup freshly squeezed tangerine juice
    (about 2 tangerines)
3 tablespoons freshly squeezed lime juice
    (about 2 limes)*

Process the cherries in a juicer. Add the tangerine and lime juices and mix well. Serve immediately.

Pineapple-Pear-Cherry Juice ▶

Watermelon-Strawberry-Red Grape Juice

Hot, steamy days seem to beg for a drink like this—tangy, light, and refreshing.

Makes about 3 cups.

1½ cups peeled and coarsely chopped watermelon
2 cups strawberries
1 cup red grapes

Process the watermelon, strawberries, and grapes in a juicer. Mix well and serve immediately.

Watermelon-Raspberry-Apple Juice

This rosy juice highlights the best flavors of summer by using juicy watermelon and plump, sweet raspberries. Apple juice acts as a neutral base for these favorite summertime fruits.

Makes about 3 cups.

1½ cups peeled and coarsely chopped watermelon
2 cups raspberries
1 apple, cut into wedges

Process the watermelon, raspberries, and apple in a juicer. Mix well and serve immediately.

Watermelon-Cherry-Nectarine Juice

This winning fruit juice is also sensational when made with ripe strawberries instead of the cherries.

Makes about 3 cups.

2½ cups peeled and coarsely chopped watermelon
1 cup pitted cherries
1 nectarine, pitted and cut into wedges

Process the watermelon, cherries, and nectarine in a juicer. Mix well and serve immediately.

Five-Fruit Juice

You can vary the five fruits in this drink according to the seasons and your fancy to make a pleasing morning tonic or afternoon snack drink. The combination of apple, tangerine, pear, grapes, and nectarine results in a juice that is frothy, slightly thick, and balanced in flavor.

Makes about 3 cups.

3 small apples, cut into wedges
1 nectarine, pitted and cut into wedges
1 small pear, cut into wedges
1 cup red grapes
½ cup freshly squeezed tangerine juice

Process the apples, nectarine, pear, and grapes in a juicer. Add the tangerine juice and mix well. Serve immediately.

Strawberry-Apple-Tangerine Juice

The sweet-tart flavor of tangerine juice has always been a favorite of mine, and I've combined it with juicy apples and strawberries to make a winning juice. A glassful will give you a good running start to the day.

Makes about 2½ cups.

10 large strawberries
2 apples, cut into wedges
1 cup freshly squeezed tangerine juice
   (about 4 tangerines)

Process the strawberries and apples in a juicer. Add the tangerine juice and mix well. Serve immediately.

Peach-Blueberry-Tangerine Juice

This striking, orange-hued fruit drink is mild and subtle and tastes like the essence of the sun-ripened fruits. This juice is best made at the height of summer, when stone fruits are at their peak.

Makes about 3 cups.

3 peaches, pitted and cut into wedges
3 plums, pitted and cut into wedges
5 apricots, pitted and cut into wedges

Process the peaches, plums, and apricots in a juicer. Mix well and serve immediately.

Strawberry-Apple-Pineapple Juice

The apple tempers the sweetness of the pineapple and strawberries in this pale pink and richly flavored juice.

Makes about 3½ cups.

2 cups strawberries
1 apple, cut into wedges
2 cups peeled and coarsely chopped pineapple
(about half a large pineapple)

Process the strawberries, apple, and pineapple in a juicer. Mix well and serve immediately.

Peach-Plum-Apricot Juice

Barely sweet, with a pleasing tart aftertaste, this pale lavender fruit juice is wonderful in the morning. Feel free to substitute nectarines for the peaches and oranges for the tangerines.

Makes about 3 cups.

3 peaches, pitted and cut into wedges
2 cups blueberries
1 cup freshly squeezed tangerine juice
(about 3 tangerines)

Process the peaches and blueberries in a juicer. Add the tangerine juice and mix well. Serve immediately.

Carrot-Green Pepper-Fennel-Bean Sprout Juice

This light and very pleasant juice combines four vegetables with very distinct tastes. The result is a harmonious blend of their wonderful flavors and is loaded with vitamins and minerals.

Makes about 2 cups.

3 carrots, trimmed
1 green pepper, cut into wedges
1 bulb fennel, trimmed and cut into wedges
2 cups bean sprouts, chopped

Process the carrots, green pepper, fennel, and bean sprouts in a juicer. Mix well and serve immediately.

Carrot-Bean Sprout-Celery-Jalapeño Juice

Choose any variety of bean sprout for this stimulating, healthful tonic. When using the larger, thicker mung bean sprouts I find it helpful to chop them coarsely before placing them in the juicer. Bean sprouts add a wonderful malty flavor to this juice.

Makes about 2 cups.

4 carrots, trimmed
2 cups bean sprouts, coarsely chopped
3 stalks celery, trimmed
2 jalapeño peppers, stemmed

Process the carrots, bean sprouts, celery, and jalapeño peppers in a juicer. Mix well and serve immediately.

Fennel-Cucumber-Sprout Juice

This vibrant green vegetable juice is very refreshing on hot summer days. Its bright, clean taste is an immediate stimulant.

Makes about 3 cups.

1 bulb fennel, trimmed and cut into wedges
1 large cucumber, peeled and cut into wedges
2 cups sprouts

Process the fennel, cucumber, and sprouts in a juicer. Mix well and serve immediately.

Snap Pea-Celery-Sprout Juice

Sweet, refreshing, and light, this is one of my favorite vegetable juices. Snap peas and sprouts don't produce vast quantities of juice, but their precious liquids are truly delectable. If you can't find snap peas, then substitute snow peas.

Makes about 1¼ cups.

2 cups snap peas
2 stalks celery, trimmed
2 cups sprouts

Process the snap peas, celery, and sprouts in a juicer. Mix well and drink immediately.

Nectarine-Strawberry-Orange Juice

Why settle for a boring glass of orange juice in the morning when you can have this refreshing beverage. It is terrific over ice as well.

Makes about 3½ cups.

2 nectarines, pitted and cut into wedges
2 cups strawberries
½ cup freshly squeezed orange juice
   (about 2 oranges)

Process the nectarines and strawberries in a juicer. Add the orange juice and mix well. Serve immediately.

Grape-Apple-Pear Juice

Serve this sweet, light fruit beverage on warm afternoons. Over ice and garnished with sprigs of mint, it is the perfect refresher.

Makes about 3 cups.

1 cup red grapes
1 apple, cut into wedges
3 pears, cut into wedges

Process the grapes, apple, and pears in a juicer. Mix well and serve immediately.

Watermelon-Nectarine-Pear Juice

Lean and delicate, this refreshing juice is a sensational thirst quencher on hot summer afternoons. Its soothing flavor would be especially appealing to children with finicky palates.

Makes about 3 cups.

2 cups peeled and coarsely chopped watermelon
2 nectarines, pitted and cut into wedges
2 pears, cut into wedges

Process the watermelon, nectarines, and pears in a juicer. Mix well and serve immediately.

Cantaloupe-Mango Juice

Pale orange in color and subtle in flavor, this juice is for those who enjoy the mild but definite flavor of cantaloupe, and the sweet, tropical taste of mango.

Makes about 2¼ cups.

1½ cups peeled and chopped cantaloupe
  (about half of a small cantaloupe)
1 mango, peeled, pitted, and cut into wedges
⅓ cup freshly squeezed lemon juice
  (about 4 lemons)

Process the cantaloupe and mango in a juicer. Add the lemon juice and mix well. Serve immediately.

Pineapple-Peach-Apple Juice

The sweetness of the pineapple and peach are balanced by the tang of apple in this delightful drink. Make it for an afternoon snack midsummer when pineapples and peaches are plentiful.

Makes about 2½ cups.

1 cup peeled and chopped pineapple
  (about one-quarter of a large pineapple)
2 peaches, pitted and cut into wedges
1 apple, cut into wedges

Process the pineapple, peaches, and apple in a juicer. Mix well and serve immediately.

Mango-Pineapple-Peach Juice

Rich and aromatic, this tropical juice is quite thick, so you may want to add a little mineral or sparkling water to thin it to your taste.

Makes about 2 cups.

1 mango, peeled, pitted, and cut into wedges
1 cup peeled and coarsely chopped pineapple
  (about one-quarter of a large pineapple)
1 peach, pitted and cut into wedges

Process the mango, pineapple, and peach in a juicer. Mix well and serve immediately.

Plum-Apple-Grape Juice

Light, refreshing, and very drinkable, yellow plums make a pale green juice that is at once tart and sweet. Feel free to use red plums if yellow are not available.

Makes about 3 cups.

2 plums, pitted and cut into wedges
1 apple, cut into wedges
2 cups green grapes

Process the plums, apple, and grapes in a juicer. Mix well and serve immediately.

Celery-Green Pepper-Parsley-Carrot Juice

This may not be the most visually appealing vegetable drink, but its vitamins, minerals, and satisying flavor more than compensate for its lackluster appearance.

Makes about 2 cups.

2 stalks celery, trimmed
2 green peppers, cut into wedges
1 bunch parsley
1 large carrot, trimmed

Process the celery, green peppers, parsley, and carrot in a juicer. Mix well and serve immediately.

Fennel-Grape-Cucumber Juice

Combining fruit with vegetables results in some surprisingly delicious juices; I suggest trying this pale green, frothy beverage mid-morning when you need a quick pick-me-up.

Makes about 2½ cups.

2 bulbs fennel, trimmed and cut into wedges
1 cup green grapes
1 small cucumber, peeled and cut into wedges

Process the fennel, grapes, and cucumber in a juicer. Mix well and serve immediately.

Carrot-Beet-Celery-Tomato Juice

This bright fuchsia-colored vegetable drink is absolutely stunning. Intensely flavored, vibrant and delicious, serve this beverage to anyone who needs a jolt of energy.

Makes about 2 cups.

2 carrots, trimmed
2 red beets, trimmed and cut into wedges
2 stalks celery, trimmed
2 tomatoes, cut into wedges

Process the carrots, beets, celery, and tomatoes in a juicer. Mix well and serve immediately.

Carrot-Tomato-Fennel-Lettuce Juice

The taste of carrots dominates this wonderful juice, but undertones of fennel and tomato create a round and balanced vegetable flavor that will hit the spot most any time.

Makes about 3 cups.

2 carrots, trimmed
3 tomatoes, cut into wedges
1 bulb fennel, trimmed and cut into wedges
10 romaine lettuce leaves, halved

Process the carrots, tomatoes, fennel, and romaine leaves in a juicer. Mix well and serve immediately.

2. Blender Drinks

Most any fruit or vegetable can be placed in a blender and puréed to a soft, smooth consistency, but, generally speaking, fruits are more commonly puréed in a blender than vegetables. The soft, juicy-sweet flesh of most fruits lends itself to this treatment and usually results in wonderfully smooth and very delicious beverages. As stated earlier, blender drinks include the fiber of whatever is being processed, so in a way these drinks are more nutritionally complete than their liquid counterparts made in a juicer. I find it's best to include an equal portion of both juice and blender drinks in my diet, of course supplementing them with whole fruits and vegetables.

Remember that fruits with hard or inedible skins, such as melons, pineapples, kiwis, and citrus fruits, must first be peeled before blending. Obviously, pits, stems, and seeds must be removed as well. Fruits with a great deal of fiber, such as mangoes or pineapples, and berries with many seeds, such as raspberries, blackberries, boysenberries, and to some extent, blueberries, produce a mixture thick with fibers or hundreds of tiny unpleasant seeds. Beverages containing these types of fruits must therefore be strained before they are served.

When using fruits that are starchy or that have a low moisture content, it's best to combine them with other fruits that are high in moisture. For example, if you blend a banana and a pear together, they produce a thick, flat-tasting sludge rather than a bright-tasting, colorful, fluid beverage. In this case, I suggest adding a few high-moisture, colorful fruits, such as apricots, plums, peaches, or perhaps some citrus juice. Many fruit combinations make very thick beverages, oftentimes too thick to drink. This may be acceptable to you, but if you want to thin the beverages so that they may be sipped like regular juices, you can add water, orange juice, tonic water, mineral water, or crushed ice cubes.

If you suspect the fruit for a given recipe is too tart, you may include a few pitted dates, and if the finished product isn't sweet enough you can add a tablespoon of honey. By and large, there aren't many rules when it comes to making delicious blender drinks—just experiment until you find pleasing combinations of texture, flavor, color, and aroma.

These blender recipes yield approximately 2½ to 3½ cups per recipe. The average portion for one person is about 10 ounces, so most of the recipes make a quantity sufficient for at least two people or for a small taste for three to four people. Many of the thick nectars can be poured over ice or extended with water to serve more than two people, and all of the recipes can be doubled or tripled with great success.

Recipes in this section are described as a nectar, fizz, cooler, or smoothie. A nectar refers to the natural, unadulterated pulp and juice resulting from puréeing several fruits together in a blender. A smoothie is a nectar to which low-fat or non-fat yogurt is added, a fizz includes sparkling water or club soda, and a cooler incorporates crushed ice. The nectars are the most basic recipes in this section, but they all can be transformed by adding one or two of the other ingredients. I added yogurt, sparkling water, or crushed ice to certain fruit combinations

based on their color, texture, consistency, and flavor. Some beverages begged for a spoonful of tart, creamy yogurt, while others wanted a splash of fizzy water. Still other combinations were elevated by a bit of crushed ice, transforming the beverage into something icy, slushy, and ultra-refreshing.

In addition to making superb and healthful beverages, many of these blender recipes can double as chilled fruit soup bases; as sauces for cakes, ice cream, or puddings; as toppings for cereal or yogurt; or as bases for festive summer cocktails. Be creative and develop you own uses for these sublime concoctions.

Strawberry-Tangerine-Pear Nectar ▶

Strawberry-Tangerine-Pear Nectar

Tart and pink, with a mild berry flavor, this subtle nectar makes a filling breakfast drink and is excellent spooned over sliced bananas and apples.

Makes about 2½ cups.

1 cup strawberries, stemmed
1 cup freshly squeezed tangerine juice
* (about 4 tangerines)*
1 pear, cored and coarsely chopped

Place the strawberries, tangerine juice, and pear in a blender. Blend until smooth. Strain through a fine wire sieve. Serve immediately.

Strawberry-Banana-Lemon Nectar

Fresh lemon juice heightens the natural sweetness and flavors of the strawberries and cuts the richness of the banana in this lovely, rose-colored nectar.

Makes about 1⅓ cups.

10 strawberries, stemmed
1 small banana, peeled and broken into pieces
¼ cup freshly squeezed lemon juice
* (1 or 2 lemons)*

Place the strawberries, banana, and lemon juice in a blender. Blend until smooth. Serve immediately.

Raspberry-Strawberry-Peach Nectar

Two summer berries make this thick, delectable beverage deep red and very sweet. For a simple sorbet-like dessert, pour this nectar into a plastic or stainless steel bowl and cover tightly. Freeze until firm and serve in small bowls for a fat-free summer dessert.

Makes about 2 cups.

1 cup raspberries
1 cup strawberries, stemmed
2 peaches, pitted and coarsely chopped

Place the raspberries, strawberries, and peaches in a blender. Blend until smooth. Strain through a fine wire sieve and serve immediately.

Raspberry-Strawberry-Peach Nectar ▶

Strawberry-Orange-Mango Nectar

This delectable nectar is superb alone, but it takes on an extra dimension when poured over ice and spiked with lemon vodka. When choosing mangoes, look for smooth-skinned fruit with resilient texture and orange-red skins.

Makes about 2 cups.

1 cup strawberries, stemmed
1 cup freshly squeezed orange juice (3 to 4 oranges)
1 mango, peeled, pitted, and coarsely chopped

Place the strawberries, orange juice, and mango in a blender. Blend until smooth. Strain through a fine wire sieve. Serve immediately.

Raspberry-Blackberry-Orange Nectar

Deep violet, this handsome, berry-infused nectar makes a fine mid-morning snack, but it also doubles as a nonfat and very flavorful dessert sauce. If the berries are not particularly ripe or sweet, you may want to add a little honey to this nectar.

Makes 3½ cups.

2 cups raspberries
2 cups blackberries
1 cup freshly squeezed orange juice (about 3 oranges)

Place the raspberries, blackberries, and orange juice in a blender. Blend until smooth. Strain through a fine wire sieve. Serve immediately.

Yellow Cherry-Papaya-Nectarine Cooler

I made this nectar with yellow cherries from my local farmer's market, and it gave the beverage a soft yellow tone that was very pretty. If you cannot find yellow cherries, the more common red ones will work just fine.

Makes about 3 cups.

2 cups pitted yellow Rainier cherries
1 papaya, peeled, pitted, and coarsely chopped
1 nectarine, pitted and coarsely chopped

Place the cherries, papaya, and nectarine in a blender. Blend until smooth. Serve immediately.

Honeydew Melon-Apricot-Nectarine Fizz

This delightful summer fruit concoction is even more stimulating when poured over crushed ice. If you prefer, you may substitute peaches for the nectarines in this drink.

Makes about 4 cups.

2 cups peeled, seeded, and coarsely chopped
*   honeydew melon (about half of a medium melon)*
2 apricots, pitted and coarsely chopped
2 nectarines, pitted and coarsely chopped
1 cup sparkling water or club soda

Place the honeydew melon, apricots, and nectarines in a blender. Blend until smooth. Add the sparkling water and mix gently. Serve immediately.

Nectarine-Apricot-Banana Nectar

Rich and thick, this orange-hued drink with flecks of red nectarine skin makes a striking beverage served in hurricane glasses over ice and thinned with a little water or vodka. It also makes a pleasing, fat-free fruit sauce for desserts.

Makes about 3 cups.

3 nectarines, pitted and coarsely chopped
3 apricots, pitted and coarsely chopped
1 banana, peeled and broken into pieces
Freshly squeezed juice of 1 lemon

Place the nectarines, apricots, banana, and lemon juice in a blender. Blend until smooth. Serve immediately.

Nectarine-Plum-Peach Juice

This beautiful, sweetly tart fruit nectar tastes like summer itself. Serve it first thing in the morning to add spark to your breakfast routine.

Makes about 3½ cups.

2 nectarines, pitted and coarsely chopped
3 plums, pitted and coarsely chopped
3 peaches, pitted and coarsely chopped

Place the nectarines, plums, and peaches in a blender. Blend until smooth. Serve immediately.

Nectarine-Peach-Apricot-Lime Nectar

Lime juice provides a tart accent to the sweet taste of three stone fruits in this agreeable drink. Add a splash of tequila and pour over crushed ice for a fruity Margarita.

Makes about 3½ cups.

2 nectarines, pitted and coarsely chopped
1 peach, pitted and coarsely chopped
3 apricots, pitted and coarsely chopped
¼ cup freshly squeezed lime juice (2 to 3 limes)

Place the nectarines, peach, apricots, and lime juice in a blender. Blend until smooth. Serve immediately.

Banana-Peach-Nectarine Smoothie

Ideal for infants, this luxurious smoothie is simple, straightforward, and made with the familiar fruits of summer. Serve it as a delicious and nutritious afternoon snack.

Makes about 2½ cups.

1 banana, peeled and broken into pieces
1 peach, pitted and coarsely chopped
1 nectarine, pitted and coarsely chopped
3 tablespoons plain low-fat yogurt

Place the banana, peach, nectarine, and yogurt in a blender. Blend until smooth. Serve immediately.

Papaya-Banana-Pineapple Fizz

Rich with the flavors of tropical fruits, this delightful beverage is creamy and satisfying. If papaya is not available, substitute peaches or mango.

Makes about 4 cups.

1 large papaya, peeled, seeded, and
  coarsely chopped
1 banana, peeled and broken into pieces
2 cups peeled and chopped pineapple
  (about half of a large pineapple)
1 cup sparkling water or club soda

Place the papaya, banana, and pineapple in blender. Blend until smooth. Strain through a fine wire sieve. Add the sparkling water and mix gently. Serve immediately.

Papaya-Watermelon-Lime Cooler

This refreshing and lively beverage reminds me of the *agua frescas* sold in Latin American restaurants. Watermelon is one of the more popular fruits used for these thin, cool drinks, but when combined with the rich flesh and sultry flavor of papaya and highlighted with a dash of fresh lime juice, this version tops all others.

Makes about 3½ cups.

1 large papaya, peeled, seeded, and
  coarsely chopped
1½ cups peeled and coarsely chopped watermelon
3 tablespoons freshly squeezed lime juice
  (about 2 limes)
Dash of salt (optional)
4 ice cubes, crushed

Place the papaya, watermelon, and lime juice in a blender. Blend just until smooth. (Over-blending will crush the watermelon seeds.) Strain through a fine wire sieve and return to the blender. Add the salt and ice cubes and blend until smooth and slushy. Serve immediately.

Peach-Plum-Ginger Cooler

At once cool, tart, sweet, and fiery, this unique blender drink is delicious on its own, but it also makes an outstanding base for a rum-spiked cocktail.

Makes about 3 cups.

3 peaches, pitted and coarsely chopped
4 small red plums, pitted and coarsely chopped
¼-inch piece fresh gingerroot, peeled
8 ice cubes, crushed

Place the peaches, plums, and ginger in a blender. Blend until smooth. Strain through a fine wire sieve and return to the blender. Add the ice cubes and purée until smooth. Serve immediately.

Blackberry-Apricot-Pineapple Cooler

Dramatically deep violet in color, this tart and exotic beverage is sure to please thirsty guests on a hot summer day. For an alcoholic variation, add a splash of light rum or vodka.

Makes about 3½ cups.

2 cups blackberries
4 apricots, pitted and coarsely chopped
½ cup peeled and chopped pineapple
  (about one-eighth of a large pineapple)
8 ice cubes, crushed

Place the blackberries, apricots, and pineapple in a blender. Blend until smooth. Strain through a fine wire sieve and return to the blender with the ice cubes. Purée until smooth and serve immediately.

Banana-Pineapple-Smoothie with Blueberries

This creamy potion, with its dark blue "dots," makes a stunning and unique drink. For a pleasing dessert, mix with 1 cup softened vanilla ice cream and freeze for 1 to 2 hours or until slightly firm.

Makes about 2 cups.

*1 cup peeled and chopped pineapple
    (about one-quarter of a large pineapple)
2 large bananas, peeled and broken into pieces
3 tablespoons plain low-fat yogurt
1 cup blueberries*

Place the pineapple, bananas, and yogurt in a blender. Blend until smooth. Strain through a fine wire sieve. Add the blueberries and mix gently. Serve immediately.

Banana-Kiwi Orange Nectar

The kiwi and orange cut the richness of the banana in this unusual nectar, making this a wonderful, not-too-sweet morning beverage.

Makes about 2 cups.

*1 banana, peeled and broken into pieces
1 kiwi, peeled and halved
1 cup freshly squeezed orange juice
    (about 3 oranges)*

Place the banana, kiwi, and orange juice in a blender. Blend until smooth. Serve immediately.

Apricot-Tangerine Smoothie

This is one of my favorite drinks; it is smooth, sweet, and comforting. To make a cooling dessert, pour into a container and place in the freezer for a couple of hours, or until very cold and semifrozen. Place in a blender along with 1 cup of vanilla ice cream and purée until smooth. Serve garnished with sprigs of mint.

Makes about 2 cups.

10 apricots, pitted and coarsely chopped
1 cup freshly squeezed tangerine juice
    (about 4 tangerines)
3 tablespoons plain low-fat yogurt

Place the apricots, tangerine juice, and yogurt in a blender. Blend until smooth and serve immediately.

Apricot-Banana-Honeydew Melon Nectar

Subtle and not too sweet, this mild nectar is best thinned with a little cold water or poured over ice for a healthful afternoon beverage.

Makes about 3 cups.

5 apricots, pitted and coarsely chopped
1 banana, peeled and broken into pieces
2 cups peeled, seeded, and coarsely chopped
    honeydew melon (about half of a medium melon)

Place the apricots, banana, and melon in a blender. Blend until smooth. Serve immediately.

Tangerine-Raspberry-Cantaloupe Smoothie

The tangy-sweet flavor of citrus, and the unmistakable flavor of raspberries meld well with the mild qualities of cantaloupe, making this a satisfying refresher any time of the day.

Makes about 2½ cups.

*½ cup freshly squeezed tangerine juice
    (about 2 tangerines)
2 cups raspberries
2 cups peeled, seeded, and coarsely chopped
    cantaloupe (about half of a large cantaloupe)
3 tablespoons plain low-fat yogurt*

Place the tangerine juice, raspberries, cantaloupe, and yogurt in a blender. Blend until smooth. Strain through a fine wire sieve and serve immediately.

Orange-Pineapple-Raspberry Fizz

This light, pale peach-colored drink is a terrific appetizer beverage. It is also quite good made with a splash of vodka.

Makes about 4 cups.

*1 cup freshly squeezed orange juice
    (3 to 4 oranges)
2 cups peeled and coarsely chopped pineapple
    (about half of a large pineapple)
1 cup raspberries
1 cup sparkling or soda water*

Place the orange juice, pineapple, and raspberries in a blender. Blend until smooth. Strain through a fine wire sieve. Add the sparkling water and mix gently. Serve immediately.

Cantaloupe-Orange-Papaya Smoothie

This creamy, brilliant orange fruit drink makes a soothing summer tonic for breakfast or lunch. It also can be frozen and served as a chilled fruit dessert.

Makes about 3½ cups.

1½ cups peeled, seeded, and coarsely chopped
  cantaloupe (about half of a small cantaloupe)
2 cups freshly squeezed orange juice (3 to 4 oranges)
1 papaya, peeled, seeded, and coarsely chopped
3 tablespoons low-fat yogurt

Place the cantaloupe, orange juice, papaya, and yogurt in a blender. Blend until smooth. Serve immediately.

Cantaloupe-Nectarine-Date Nectar

Dates have a dense texture and intense, earthy sweetness, and when combined with the mild flavor of cantaloupe and sweet-tart nectarines, the result is simply divine. This pale orange beverage is wonderful as a mid-afternoon snack or after-dinner dessert drink.

Makes about 2 cups.

2 cups peeled, seeded, and coarsely chopped
  cantaloupe (about half of a large cantaloupe)
2 nectarines, pitted and coarsely chopped
⅓ cup pitted dates (about 15 dates)

Place the cantaloupe, nectarines, and dates in a blender. Blend until smooth. Serve immediately.

Peach-Grape Nectar

It's hard to believe that two such simple, common fruits could make such a tasty drink, but this combination is one of my favorites. Rich, filling, and thick, this juice is almost a meal in itself.

Makes about 2 cups.

1 large peach, pitted and coarsely chopped
2 cups seedless green grapes

Place the peach and grapes in a blender. Blend until smooth. Strain through a fine wire sieve. Serve immediately.

Peach-Grapefruit-Banana Nectar

Grapefruit juice adds just the right note of tartness to this sweet and substantial beverage.

Makes about 2 cups.

2 peaches, pitted and coarsely chopped
½ cup freshly squeezed grapefruit juice
    (about 1 grapefruit)
2 bananas, peeled and broken into pieces

Place the peaches, grapefruit juice, and bananas in a blender. Blend until smooth. Serve immediately.

Banana-Papaya-Lemon Cooler

Tropical and luscious, this cool, creamy beverage would be a perfect drink to sip while lounging by the pool.

Makes about 2½ cups.

1 banana, peeled and broken into pieces
1 papaya, peeled, seeded, and coarsely chopped
¼ cup freshly squeezed lemon juice
    (about 3 lemons)
8 ice cubes, crushed

Place the banana, papaya, and lemon juice in a blender. Blend until smooth. Add the ice cubes and purée until smooth. Serve immediately.

Pineapple-Banana-Tangerine Nectar

There's nothing like the taste of fresh pineapple, and when it is combined with the other fruits in this pale yellow nectar, it makes waking up seem much more appealing.

Makes about 3 cups.

2 cups peeled and coarsely chopped pineapple
    (about half of a large pineapple)
1 banana, peeled and broken into pieces
1 cup freshly squeezed tangerine juice
    (about 4 tangerines)

Place the pineapple, banana, and tangerine juice in a blender. Blend until smooth. Strain if desired and serve immediately.

85

Papaya-Tangerine Nectar

A brilliant orange color combined with bright flavors and a silky texture make this one of most pleasing drinks in this collection.

Makes about 2 cups.

1 large papaya, peeled, seeded, and coarsely chopped
1 cup freshly squeezed tangerine juice
  (about 4 tangerines)

Place the papaya and tangerine juice in a blender. Blend until smooth. Serve immediately.

Mango-Peach Smoothie

The skins from the peach give this sunny beverage an interesting texture and color. Although the recipe calls for plain yogurt, try adding vanilla-flavored yogurt for a different flavor.

Makes about 3 cups.

1 mango, peeled, pitted, and coarsely chopped
3 peaches, pitted and coarsely chopped
3 tablespoons low-fat yogurt

Place the mango, peaches, and yogurt in a blender. Blend until smooth. Strain through a fine wire mesh and serve immediately.

Cantaloupe-Peach-Strawberry Nectar

Serve this pale pink sweetie in tall glasses over ice. It's a perfect way to start—or end—the day.

Makes about 3½ cups.

*1½ cups peeled and coarsely chopped cantaloupe
(about half of a small cantaloupe)
1 peach, pitted and coarsely chopped
1½ cups strawberries, stemmed*

Place the cantaloupe, peach, and strawberries in a blender. Blend until smooth. Strain through a fine wire sieve and serve immediately.

Tangerine-Nectarine-Strawberry Fizz

This inviting fruit drink has a pleasing citrus flavor. Serve it in a tall glass and garnish with whole strawberries for a festive brunch drink.

Makes about 3½ cups.

*1 cup freshly squeezed tangerine juice
(about 4 tangerines)
2 nectarines, pitted and coarsely chopped
10 strawberries, stemmed
1 cup sparkling water*

Place the tangerine juice, nectarines, and straw-berries in a blender. Blend until smooth. Strain through a fine wire sieve. Add the sparkling water and mix well. Serve immediately.

Kiwi-Honeydew Melon Nectar

This slightly peppery fruit drink has an unusual, almost crunchy texture from the tiny seeds in the kiwi fruit. Poured over ice and garnished with fresh mint, this pale green beverage would be a good antidote for a hot summer day.

Makes about 2 cups.

2 kiwi, peeled and halved
2 cups peeled and coarsely chopped honeydew melon
    (about half of a medium melon)

Place the kiwi and melon in a blender. Blend until smooth. Serve immediately.

Banana-Nectarine-Apricot-Tangerine Nectar

Four fruits lend their distinctive and delicious flavors to this nectar. What better way to start the day?

Makes about 2½ cups.

1 banana, peeled and broken into pieces
1 nectarine, pitted and coarsely chopped
2 apricots, pitted and coarsely chopped
¾ cup freshly squeezed tangerine juice
    (about 3 tangerines)

Place the banana, nectarine, apricots, and tangerine juice in a blender. Blend until smooth. Serve immediately.

Blueberry-Banana-Date-Lemon Fizz

This is one of my favorite indulgences. Sweet, thick, and dessert-like, this complex-tasting concoction takes on a refreshing and effervescent quality when mixed with the sparkling water.

Makes about 3½ cups.

2 cups blueberries
2 bananas, peeled and broken into pieces
⅓ cup chopped and pitted dates (about 15 dates)
¼ cup freshly squeezed lemon juice
    (about 2 lemons)
1 cup sparkling water or club soda

Place the blueberries, bananas, dates, and lemon juice in a blender. Blend until smooth. Add the sparkling water and mix gently. Serve immediately.

Blueberry-Blackberry-Peach Nectar

The berries can be varied according to what is available, so if you have a particular favorite, feel free to substitute.

Makes about 3½ cups.

2 cups blueberries
1 cup blackberries
2 peaches, pitted and coarsely chopped

Place the blueberries, blackberries, and peaches in a blender. Blend until smooth. Strain through a fine wire sieve and serve immediately.

Blueberry-Kiwi-Peach Nectar

This unusual trio of fruits results in a deep violet juice that makes a wonderful sauce drizzled over cake, ice cream, or fresh fruit.

Makes about 3½ cups.

2 cups blueberries
1 kiwi, peeled and halved
1 peach, pitted and coarsely chopped

Place the blueberries, kiwi, and peach in a blender. Blend until smooth. Strain through a fine wire sieve and serve immediately.

Cherry-Pear-Peach Nectar

A cherry pitter will make fast work of the preparation for this rosy pink nectar. Served over ice, it makes an excellent thirst quencher.

Makes about 2½ cups.

1 cup pitted cherries
1 pear, cored and coarsely chopped
1 large peach, pitted and coarsely chopped

Place the cherries, pear, and peach in a blender. Blend until smooth. Serve immediately.

Honeydew Melon-Peach-Apricot Smoothie

A creamy smooth texture and pleasant flavor make this a winning beverage to savor in the morning or at the end of a long day.

Makes about 3 cups.

2 cups peeled and coarsely chopped honeydew melon (about half of a medium melon)
1 peach, pitted and coarsely chopped
3 apricots, pitted and coarsely chopped
3 tablespoons low-fat yogurt

Place the honeydew melon, peach, apricots, and yogurt in the blender. Blend until smooth. Serve immediately.

Apricot-Raspberry-Cherry Smoothie

Raspberries and cherries both have vivid red color and sweetly tart flavor; when paired with ripe apricots and yogurt, the result is a drink that is as pleasing to the palate as to the eye.

Makes about 2½ cups.

2 apricots, pitted and coarsely chopped
1 cup raspberries
2 cups pitted cherries
3 tablespoons low-fat yogurt

Place the apricots, raspberries, cherries, and yogurt in a blender. Blend until smooth. Strain through a fine wire sieve and serve immediately.

Apricot-Orange-Pear Cooler

Bright, citrusy, and invigorating, serve this fruit beverage for a cooling afternoon treat.

Makes about 3 cups.

4 apricots, pitted and coarsely chopped
1 cup freshly squeezed orange juice
  (about 3 oranges)
1 pear, cored and coarsely chopped
8 ice cubes, crushed

Place the apricots, orange juice, and pear in a blender. Blend until smooth. Add the crushed ice and purée until smooth. Serve immediately.

Table of Equivalents

The exact equivalents in the following tables have been rounded for convenience.

US/UK	METRIC	US	METRIC	UK
oz=ounce	g=gram	2 tbl	30 ml	1 fl oz
lb=pound	kg=kilogram	1/4 cup	60 ml	2 fl oz
in=inch	mm=millimeter	1/3 cup	80 ml	3 fl oz
ft=foot	cm=centimeter	1/2 cup	125 ml	4 fl oz
tbl=tablespoon	ml=milliliter	2/3 cup	160 ml	5 fl oz
fl oz=fluid ounce	l=liter	3/4 cup	180 ml	6 fl oz
qt=quart		1 cup	250 ml	8 fl oz
		1 1/2 cups	375 ml	8 fl oz